What do we think about

Our Environment?

Malcolm Penny

HODDER
Wayland

an imprint of Hodder Children's Books

Titles in the series

What do we think about …

Adoption • Alcohol • Bullying
Death • Disability • Drugs
Family Break-Up • Our Environment

All Hodder Wayland books encourage children to read and help them improve their literacy.

✓ The contents page, page numbers, headings and index help locate specific pieces of information.

✓ The glossary reinforces alphabetic knowledge and extends vocabulary.

✓ The further information section suggests other books dealing with the same subject.

✓ Find out more about how this book is specifically relevant to the National Literacy Strategy on page 31.

Editor: Elizabeth Gogerly
Consultant: John Bennett, a Health Education Coordinator
Cover designer: Jan Sterling
Designer: Jean Wheeler
Photo researcher/stylist: Gina Brown
Production controller: Carol Titchener

First published in Great Britain in 1999
by Wayland (Publishers) Ltd
Reprinted in 2000 by Hodder Wayland,
an imprint of Hodder Children's Books

© Hodder Wayland 1999

British Library Cataloguing in Publication Data

Penny, Malcolm
What do we think about our environment?
1. Conservation of natural resources – Juvenile literature
I. Title II. Our environment
333. 7 ' 2

ISBN 0 7502 2491 6

Printed and bound in Italy byEurografica S.p.a.

Picture acknowledgements
Martyn F. Chillmaid cover (*main*), 4, 21, 26; Dennis Day cover (*background*); Ecoscene/ Ian Beames 6, /Frank Blackburn 17; ESA/PLI/Science Library 27; Eye Ubiquitous/ Roger Chester 19; Sally and Richard Greenhill 20, 25; Angela Hampton 7, 9, 10 (*top, bottom*), 11 (*top, bottom*), 12, 13, 14, 15, 16, 22, 23, 24; Tony Stone 8, 14, 18; Topham 5.

Contents

What is the environment?

The environment is all of the world we live in. It includes the air we breathe, the water we drink or swim in, the countryside around us, and the towns and cities where we live.

Today, the environment has some big problems. In some big cities the air is so dirty that people wear special masks.

What are the problems?

The whole world is getting warmer. This is called global warming. Air has also become polluted with chemicals.

Our factories and cars, and some of the everyday things that we do, have all helped to make these changes to the air we breathe.

These changes have caused other problems.
The harmful rays of the sun can now reach
us through the air.

You can use sun cream or wear clothes to
protect yourself from the sun.

What else damages our environment?

Even small actions can harm our environment. Dropping litter, painting graffiti on walls or making unnecessary noise all make life unpleasant for other people.

Little things, such as leaving the TV on stand-by at night or leaving a light on that you don't need, waste electricity too.

If everyone thought about these things, life could be better for us all.

Samantha always keeps her sweet wrappers in her pocket until she finds a bin to put them in.

How can we start to help?

The changes in the atmosphere are caused by industry and burning fuel. We buy the things industry makes, and burn fuel to travel in our cars and to heat our homes.

Samantha and her friends decided to put their jumpers on rather than leave the fire burning.

Vanessa and her parents walk with their shopping rather than using the car.

We cannot change everything we buy, or stop using fuel, but we can think about the choices we make, and their effect on the environment.

What can we do with rubbish?

A lot of things are thrown away while they are still useful. Machines can sometimes be repaired instead of being replaced. Glass, plastic, tin and paper can all be recycled.

Jim and Oliver collect bottles and jars and take them to the bottle bank to be recycled.

Jim and Oliver also collect newspapers
and magazines at school.

How can we encourage recycling?

Paper towels, writing paper, envelopes, paper cups and many other things are marked with a sign showing that they are made from paper that has been used before.

When we go shopping we can look for this symbol and choose to buy recycled products.

Jim and Oliver hunt along the shelves until they find recycled kitchen rolls.

They tell their dad that it is eco-friendly to buy these kitchen rolls.

What else can we do when we go shopping?

Refilling washing powder containers and shampoo bottles saves plastic. Using our own bags or baskets instead of supermarket bags also saves plastic.

Sally and Damon use their own shopping bags when they go shopping with their mother.

Labels tell us if the contents are eco-friendly. If we buy things made from wood, we can make sure they are from trees that will be replanted.

How can we save water?

The underground water supply is running out. Rain does not refill it properly, because too much runs off from roads and car-parks instead of soaking into the ground.

We can save water in many ways, such as by taking a shower instead of a bath, or by turning the tap off while cleaning our teeth.

How can we save fuel?

We can save fuel by using public transport. One train or bus moves more people than lots of cars. We can also share car journeys with people we know.

If we want to make a short journey, to school
or the shops, we could walk or ride a bike.
Sean and Natalie's mum always rides her bike
with them to school.

Can we stop pollution?

Gases from aerosols and old refrigerators can also pollute the atmosphere. Old refrigerators can be sent away to be safely emptied. New refrigerators use safer gases.

We can also use pump-action sprays instead of aerosols. John's dad used aerosol polish but John told him this wasn't eco-friendly.

Now John's dad always uses pump-action sprays to polish or clean the house. His mum uses pump-action hair spray too.

Can we help trees, plants and animals?

It is better to dig up weeds, because chemical weed killers can harm wildlife. Planting a tree at school will provide a home for birds and insects.

Anna and her mum made a bird table at home. The birds like to eat household scraps.

Daniel's class helped to clean out a pond.
Instead of rubbish they can now watch
fish and dragonflies.

Our wonderful world

A clean environment is good for everyone. Towns, cities and the countryside can all be beautiful, if we look after them.

Small city parks and big National Parks make life better for everybody, and for plants and animals, too.

If everyone helps in a small way, we can solve the problems that threaten our environment and the world.

Notes for parents and teachers

Read this book with children one to one or in groups. Ask them what they like best about their immediate environment, and what they think could be improved.

Discuss with them how many different kinds of environment there are, from large to small. Newspapers often write about the Earth as a planet: this can be confusing to young people. Try starting on a much smaller scale, inside the home or, where possible, the garden.

Even in large cities, parks and public spaces provide examples of shared environments. Visit these places together and try discussing what individuals can do to make life more pleasant for others. A railway station or a bus terminus offers the chance to watch how people behave – as well as giving a demonstration of air pollution by fumes and smoke from petrol.

Talk about choices in shops and supermarkets. Compare tissues or stationery made from recycled paper, for example, with those made from new materials. If the latter are found to be better, is the small loss of quality a price worth paying to protect the environment?

Environmental groups will be happy to supply information about their activities. Discuss with the children what each group does, and whether it would be worth joining. Many of these organizations work at a local level, giving the chance to go along to watch what they do.

Encourage children to take an interest in the variety of living things that share our world. How many kinds of grass, or beetles, or wild flowers can we find in a garden or a park? It is not important at this stage to know the names of all the different kinds, but to observe that they are different.

Schools can encourage an understanding of simple ecology by setting up a flower garden, or growing a few vegetables such as beans or radishes. Let the children discover what these plants need to grow, and extend the discussion to the wider world. This will also open up questions of organic farming as against the use of chemical weed killers and pesticides.

Use stories in the press or on television to start discussions about the place of wildlife in the human world. The proposed introduction of wolves into certain areas in the US, or the release of mink from fur farms in the UK are good recent examples. TV wildlife documentaries also offer a good starting point for these discussions, for example on the role of predators, or the effects of fencing agricultural land.

The principal aim of this book is to show that small actions by individuals are as effective as major international agreements in helping to protect our environment.

Glossary

atmosphere The layer of air that covers the Earth.

eco-friendly Something that does not harm the environment.

fuel Petrol, diesel, coal and gas are all fuels.

graffiti Things like people's names or rude words written or painted on walls.

industry All the companies that make things in factories.

polluted Made dirty.

public transport Trains and buses that can be used by everybody.

recycled Used again or made into something new instead of being thrown away.

Further information

Books to read

Atlas of Earth Care by Miles Litvinoff (Gaia Books, 1996)

Clean Air, Dirty Air by Lynne Pratchett (A&C Black, 1993)

Earth Words – A Dictionary of the Environment by Seymour Simon (Harper Collins, 1995)

Geography Starts Here: Your Environment by Brenda Williams (Wayland, 1995)

Organizations to contact

Greenpeace
Canonbury Villas, London, N1 2PN
Tel: 0171 865 8100

Friends of the Earth
26-28 Underwood Street, London N1 7JQ
Tel: 0171 354 5100

Use this book for teaching literacy

This book can help you in the literacy hour in the following ways:

✓ Children can discuss the themes and link them to their own experiences of the environment.

✓ They can discuss the case studies and speculate about how they might behave in each situation.

✓ They can compare this book with fictional stories about our environment to show how similar information can be presented in different ways.

✓ They can try rewriting some of the situations described in the form of a story.

Index